Dear Readers,

My goal for "Teeias Learns About Medicines" is to ed[ucate] that are historical to my son's Blackfoot culture. It is [a] means to renew access to these important plants. Many Indigenous families have lost their traditional knowledge or even their traditional resources. I believe learning about gardening and tapping into resources available may revitalize this connection as well as help with biodiversity.

Some of the plants featured in this book have been provided by Wild About Flowers – Native Alberta Wildflowers, Plants & Seeds – www.wildaboutflowers.ca

Jennie

Jennie is a Child and Youth Care Counsellor based in Alberta, Canada. Having worked in the social services field for 15 years, she took a hiatus to raise her two boys at home, while also creating and running an established day home.

This new adventure allowed her to see the world through much smaller eyes than the teenagers she typically worked with. This new insight propelled her passion for photography and telling the stories of her boys' Blackfoot culture.

Jennie is also a gardening, photography, quilting & sewing hobbyist.

JENNIE EAGLESPEAKER

My name is Teeias (tee-eye-us) and I am a Blackfoot First Nations boy

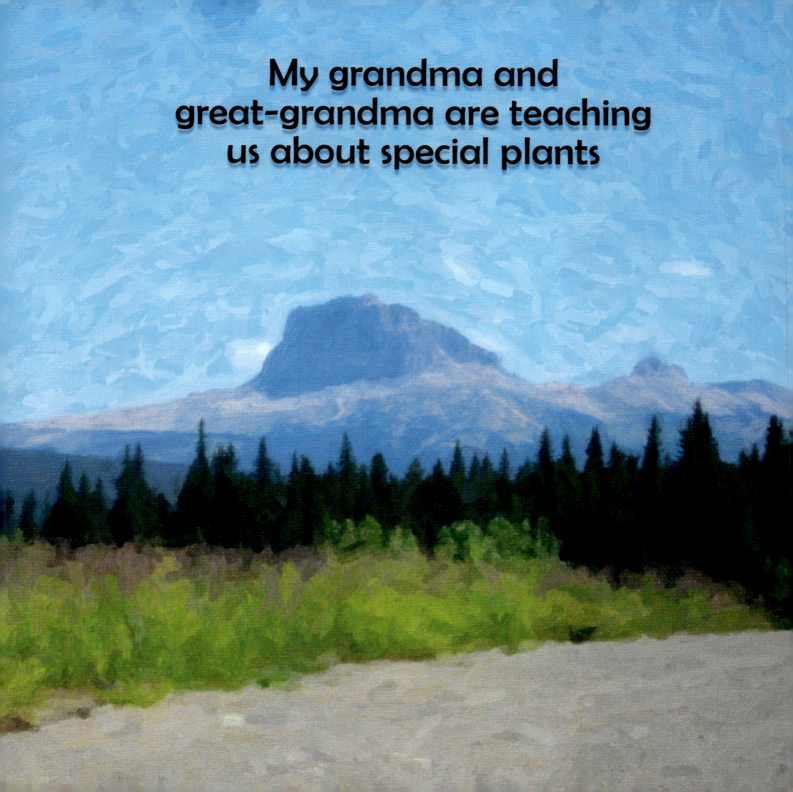

My grandma and great-grandma are teaching us about special plants

When we learn we can carry on family traditions

My family travels far to spend the day together picking

There are a lot of fascinating bugs to look at

The grasshoppers are huge and leap off our hands

Before we begin grandma teaches us how to make an offering

We will use it for tea when we are sick

She tells us about picking as a child and listening to great-grandma sing

Great-grandma watches over us, telling stories

I grow mint, sage, and yarrow in my garden

My yarrow is pink and purple but it is still the same medicine

There are many more medicines to learn about, but on another day

Dedication

To the late Leona Guardipee-EagleSpeaker ... we have all learned so much from you, we will remember and carry on your teachings.

MORE FROM EAGLESPEAKER PUBLISHING

AUTHENTICALLY INDIGENOUS GRAPHIC NOVELS:
UNeducation: A Residential School Graphic Novel
Napi the Trixster: A Blackfoot Graphic Novel
UNeducation, Vol 2

AUTHENTICALLY INDIGENOUS COLORING BOOKS:
Napi: A Coloring Experience
UNeducation: A Coloring Experience
Completely Capricious Coloring Collection
A Day at the Powwow (grayscale coloring)

AUTHENTICALLY INDIGENOUS KIDS BOOKS:
Teeias Goes To A Powwow

AUTHENTICALLY INDIGENOUS NAPI CHILDREN'S BOOKS:
Napi and the Rock
Napi and the Bullberries
Napi and the Wolves
Napi and the Buffalo
Napi and the Chickadees
Napi and the Coyote
Napi and the Elk
Napi and the Gophers
Napi and the Mice
Napi and the Prairie Chickens
Napi and the Bobcat
... and many more to come

www.eaglespeaker.com

If you absolutely loved this book (or even just kind of liked it), please find it on amazon.com and leave a quick review. Your words help more than you may realize

Made in the USA
Monee, IL
20 September 2019